Westminster Abbey

A tour of the Nave with a difference

Tony Willoughby

ISBN 978-1-78222-639-0

Book design, layout and production management by Into Print

www.intoprint.net

+44 (0)1604 832149

Westminster Abbey
A tour of the Nave with a difference

All net proceeds will go to the Dean and Chapter of Westminster

SACRED TO THE MEMORY OF
REAR ADMIRAL SIR GEORGE HOPE. K.C.B.
ERECTED BY SEVERAL CAPTAINS OF THE ROYAL NAVY
WHO SERVED UNDER HIM AS MIDSHIPMEN.

Admiral George Hope – see page 6 overleaf

Westminster Abbey
A tour of the Nave with a difference

W e are embarking on a tour of the Nave of the Abbey and are standing just inside the Great West Door facing east. We have told our tour guide that we already know all the basic background history of the Abbey and its principal 'residents' – a brave claim – and that we want to be entertained by stories that we have not heard before. We shall be walking down the North Aisle as far as the Choir Screen, then back up the Central Aisle, before turning east down the South Aisle to the gates at the South Choir Aisle.

Our guide starts with a question: "Where is the 'Prison House of Death'?" We are encouraged to look to our left towards the stained glass window in the North West tower honouring **Richard Trevithick** (1771-1833), the steam engine pioneer. A huge monument to **Captain James Montagu** (1752-1794), who died at the Battle of the Glorious First of June, obstructs our view. The monument behind Montagu is the 'Prison House of Death' erected to mark the passing of **Henry Vassal Fox, 3rd Baron Holland** (1773-1840), a senior politician in the first half of the 19th century. A nephew of Charles James Fox, whose memorial is nearby, he was, like his uncle, a leading abolitionist. His son gave instructions that the monument was to bear no inscription - one wonders why the Dean agreed. The Abbey website tells us that the monument is often referred to as the 'Prison House of Death' *as it consists of a tall tomb with a closed doorway with life size mourning figures in front, surmounted by a bust."*

Nearby on the window shelf on the west wall is a memorial to **Thomas Arnold** (1795-1842), the famous 19th century headmaster of Rugby School. He was a friend of his former pupil, **Dean Stanley**, who wrote *The Historical Memorials of Westminster Abbey* and is buried in Henry VII's Chapel.

Also on that West Wall is a memorial to **Admiral George Hope** (1767-1818) (unmarked grave in the Nave), who was one of Nelson's frigate captains at the Battle of Trafalgar. Hope saw action earlier in the French Revolutionary Wars. In 1799 he was captain of one of four ships which intercepted and captured a Spanish treasure fleet. On taking their prizes back to Plymouth, the prize money was calculated at £40,730.18s. for each captain, which could be as much as £2m in today's money.

Moving to our left into the North Aisle of the Nave we find the series of windows executed by **Sir Ninian Comper** (1864-1960) in the early part of the 20th century. Each window features two large figures, the left-hand figure being a Sovereign of significance to the development of the Church and alongside him the principal Abbot of his reign. At the foot of most of the windows is the name of an engineer. The third window along from the Trevithick window features King Henry III and Abbot Richard de Ware and honours **Charles Algernon Parsons** (1854-1931). A pioneer in the development of marine turbines, he had difficulty convincing the naval authorities that they were worth adopting for warships. He dealt with the problem by fitting out his *Turbinia* with one of his turbines and taking it through the fleet moored at Spithead for Queen Victoria's Diamond Jubilee Naval Review. He was chased by various Navy vessels, but none of them could catch him. His boat travelling at 34 knots was 7 knots faster than anything the Navy had to offer. The demonstration was a huge success. Virtually every warship thereafter was fitted with steam turbines of his invention. It is suspected that the 'demonstration' had the support of Vice Admiral Sir John Fisher, who had appreciated the urgent need for the Navy to adopt Parsons' steam turbines. His company is now a division of Siemens.

In the floor below, next to the grave of **John Hunter** (1728-1793) "The Father of Scientific Surgery" lies (actually he stands vertically) **Ben Jonson** (1574-1637), the poet, playwright and actor. The story goes that he approached the King (Charles I) and asked a favour of him. "*What is it?*" said the King. "*A plot of ground eighteen inches square*". "*Where?*" said the King. "*In Westminster Abbey*" came the reply. Why he elected for a vertical burial is not known for certain. Some say that he could not afford a horizontal space, others that he wanted to be ready for the Resurrection. The original stone, moved when the Nave was re-paved in 1834, sits at the base of the wall. The "*O Rare*" in the inscription is a pun on 'orare', the Latin for "to pray", and Shakespeare was said to have called him "*my rare Ben*". **Sir William Davenant** (1606-1668), whose grave is to be found in the South Transept, is said to have arranged for the inscription and a similar one for himself.

Charles Algernon Parsons (extract from stained glass window)

Continuing eastwards down the Aisle we cross the grave of **Sir Ninian Comper** (*supra*). In the next bay, high up on the window ledge is a monument to **Spencer Perceval** (1762-1812), the Prime Minister who was assassinated in the House of Commons. Below is the memorial to **Dr Richard Mead** (1673-1754), a physician and collector of books and art. In 1702 Mead published his first work, *A Mechanical Account of Poisons*, stating that mathematical learning would soon distinguish a physician from a quack. The work included a discussion of venomous snakes. He dissected several vipers and accurately described the mechanism of the fang and its operation, confirming that a puncture wound was necessary for the venom to take effect, in part by swallowing a sample of venom without ill effect. He was elected a physician to St Thomas' Hospital in 1703 and appointed a Governor of the hospital in 1715. Another of the Governors was Sir Thomas Guy, a bookseller, who was one of the few who made a fortune out of the South Sea Bubble. Mead encouraged Guy to use his fortune to found a hospital over the road from St Thomas' to take incurable patients discharged from St Thomas'[1].

---

1   at that time St Thomas' Hospital was in St Thomas' Street by London Bridge Station

Dr Richard Mead

He published important works on preventing the spread of plague and successfully conducted smallpox inoculation trials on condemned prisoners at Newgate prison. Mead's home was on the site now occupied by the Great Ormond Street Hospital.

A friend of Mead's, **Dr John Freind** (1675-1728)[2], was committed to the Tower in 1723 for his Jacobite sympathies. Mead took over his caseload, but paid to Freind on his release the fees which Mead received from Freind's patients during Freind's incarceration. Indeed, Freind's release from prison is said to have been prompted by Mead's refusal to prescribe for one of his patients while Freind remained in the Tower, the patient in question being the Prime Minister, **Robert Walpole** (1676-1745).

On the column to our right is the Nave pulpit, an early 16th century hexagonal pulpit from which it is said that **Archbishop Thomas Cranmer** (1489-1556) preached at the coronation of **King Edward VI**.

In the floor ahead of us there is the readily identifiable grave of **Samuel Smith** (c.1732-1808), Head Master of Westminster School and an Abbey prebendary, but just to the north of that grave is a very small and barely legible stone inscribed "*Mrs J Morris*". It was a replacement stone placed following the repaving of the Nave in 1834. The original full-size gravestone bore the following inscription:

> "*Here lie the remains of* **Genl. Staats Long Morris,** *who died 2nd April 1800 aged 70. Also Mrs Jane Morris, widow of the above, who died 15th March 1801 aged 52.*"

Presumably, post-1834 there would have been a neighbouring stone naming the general. He is of particular interest in that he is believed to be the only American buried in the Abbey itself, although another American, **William Rutherfurd,** who was from North Carolina and was another of Nelson's frigate captains at Trafalgar is buried in St Margaret's. The General was born in New York in 1728. His grandfather was **Lewis Morris** (1671-1746), one time chief justice

---

2   memorial alongside that of Congreve (*infra*)

of New York and royal governor of New Jersey. Staats Long Morris joined the British army and rose to the rank of General. Eyebrows were raised in polite society when in 1756 he married **Catherine Gordon**, Dowager Duchess of Gordon (1718-1779), but according to the *English Chronicle* he:

> *"conducted himself in this new exaltation with so much moderation, affability and friendship, that the family soon forgot the degradation the Duchess had been guilty of by such a connexion, and received her spouse into their perfect favour and esteem."*

Through that connection he acquired significant political influence and obtained permission to raise his own regiment, the 89th Highlanders (also known as "**the Gordon Highlanders**"). His final appointment was as Governor of Quebec, but it was a sinecure and he remained in England. His brother, **Lewis Morris** (1726-1798), was one of the signatories to the American Declaration of Independence.

Moving east by a couple of yards we arrive at a dividing line at the end of the first bay west of the Choir. The dividing line is readily to be seen in the decoration of the stonework above the columns (diaper work to the east and plain stone to the west). It marks the limit of Henry III's building in 1272. What was left of the Nave of the Confessor's church continued westwards. It must have looked very strange. While every effort was made to continue the style of Henry's church down the full length of the Nave, the cost of continuing the diaper work proved prohibitive.

In that last bay of the Nave to be completed in Henry's lifetime, there is much to be seen. There is a 13th century painted shield in the outer wall arcade. Similar shields appear in all the wall arcades from the East end of each Choir Aisle (north and south) until this dividing line at the end of the first bay west of the Choir. They feature the shields of the dignitaries who were of assistance to Henry in the building of the Church and are in order of seniority from east to west. The shield in this bay is that of William de Forz, Count of Aumale, the father of Avelina whose marriage to Henry III's younger son, Edmund Crouchback, in 1269 was the first Royal Wedding in Henry's church[3].

In this area we are standing among the greatest scientists of their age. In the South Wall of the next bay in the North Choir Aisle is an array of plaques honouring **Hooker**, **Wallace**, **Lister**, **Couch Adams**, **Stokes**, **Joule**, **Ramsay** and **Darwin**. In the floor of this bay of the North Aisle are memorials or graves to **Florey**, **Darwin** and the **Herschels** (William and John). Moving into the Nave we cross **Hawking**, **Clerk-Maxwell**, **Dirac**, **Faraday**, **Newton**, **Green**, **Kelvin**, **Rutherford** and **JJ Thomson**[4].

The Latin inscription on the memorial stone for **William Herschel** (1735-1822) translates: *"He broke through the confines of the heavens. Buried elsewhere"*, and reflects his fame as an amateur astronomer (he discovered Uranus) and telescope manufacturer. However, he came to this country from Germany as a gifted musician and composer. His compositions included twenty four symphonies amid a plethora of concertos, sonatas and other works. Mozart, Haydn and Beethoven are all said to have spoken highly of his compositions.

In touring the Abbey it is helpful both for the entertainment of the visitors (and for memory retention on the part of the guide) to look for links between the various individuals/topics. Thus, in this small area we embrace six Nobel Laureates, no fewer than thirteen Copley

---

3   the tombs of both Avelina and Edmund are to the North of the High Altar

4   the graves of JJ Thomson and Ernest Rutherford are usually covered by the Nave Altar

Medallists[5] and four Lucasian Professors of Mathematics[6].

One member of this select group, the second Lucasian Professor of Mathematics, was **Sir Isaac Newton** (1642-1727). Legend has it that in addition to his many other inventions, his prodigious creative output included the cat-flap, something necessitated by his cat's persistent scratching at his door. There is a cat nearby[7], but not Newton's. It is depicted at the feet of Dick Whittington in the bottom left-hand corner of the Henry V/Abbot William Colchester window (above Darwin's grave) commemorating **William Thomson, Lord Kelvin** (1824-1907). In the second decade of the 15th century **Sir Richard Whittington** (c.1354-1423) was Henry V's receiver-general of the funds for completion of the Nave; hence his presence in the window. Sadly, rather deeper research has led to the probability that not only is it most unlikely that Newton did in fact invent the cat-flap, but worse still that there is little or no evidence that either he or Whittington possessed a cat.

While on the topic of cats, it is worth noting that there is a mouse nearby on the Barham Candlesticks, the gilded wooden candlesticks carved by Robert "Mouseman" Thompson, noted for including mice in his work. The Nave Altar candlesticks honour the crew of *HMS Barham*, torpedoed off Alexandria in 1941.

Newton's monument shows a cherub pouring coins out of a bowl. This is intended to illustrate his role as Warden and then Master of the Royal Mint. He was employed at the Mint for the last 30 years

5   The Copley Medal is awarded by the Royal Society for *"outstanding achievements in research in any branch of science."*

6   Elsewhere in the Abbey there are memorials to and/or graves of four other Nobel Laureates, thirteen other Copley Medallists and one other Lucasian Professor of mathematics.

7   In fact there is another one, but a bit further away and only visible with binoculars – a gargoyle on the East face of the North West Tower depicting 'Biggles' an Abbey cat of the 1990s

of his life, much of his time being spent wandering around the inns of the City of London checking on the authenticity of the coinage passing across their counters. That said, it is fair to say that while at the Mint he supervised our move from the silver standard to the gold standard and improved the efficiency of the Mint a hundred-fold.

In the monument Newton is shown leaning on his books, one of which was his greatest work *Philosophia Naturalis Principia Mathematica* (*1686-7*). **Edmund Halley** (1656-1742)[8], President of the Royal Society, had promised Newton that the Society would publish the work at its expense. However, when Newton presented it for publication, it turned out that the Society had already spent its budget publishing another book, so Halley paid for it out of his own pocket. Strangely, the other book was on fishing.

Between the graves of Newton and Darwin lie the ashes of **Stephen Hawking** (1942-2018). His stone features a design of a black hole and an equation. Unsurprisingly the question on the mind of most visitors is: "*What does the equation mean?*" Hawking has made it easy for us. His simple explanation is that the larger the mass of a black hole, the lower the temperature of the Hawking radiation. He discovered that black holes are not entirely black in that they emit radiation now known as Hawking radiation.

Close by is a memorial stone to the great theoretical physicist, **Paul Dirac** (1902-1984), which also features an equation. It is said to be a beautiful mathematical equation, which is consistent with both the principles of quantum mechanics, an area in which he was a leading pioneer, and Einstein's theory of special relativity. It predicted the existence of anti-matter and was published in 1928 when he was only 26. He was a very strange man. Indeed, his biography by Graham Farmelo is entitled *The Strangest Man*.

---

8   memorialized in the South Cloister

Whittington and his cat

Ric Whitingtõ

HERE LIES WHAT WAS MORTAL OF

$$T = \frac{hc^3}{8\pi GMk}$$

STEPHEN HAWKING
1942-2018

1902
P.A.M
DIRAC om
PHYSICIST
$$i\hbar \cdot \partial \psi = m\psi$$
1984

He was taciturn to an extraordinary degree. It was said of him that he never used one word when no words would do. He spent most of his career at Cambridge but moved to the University of Florida when he was in his seventies. The head of the Physics department at that university was criticised by some of his colleagues for recruiting such an old and strange man to the department. His response was that it was the equivalent of the head of the English department recruiting William Shakespeare. Dirac is the only member of this distinguished group of scientists to have held the position of Lucasian Professor of Mathematics at Cambridge University and to have been awarded the Copley Medal and a Nobel Prize, although it has to be recognised that neither the Nobel Prize nor the Copley Medal were available when Newton was alive.

A near contemporary of Dirac, who attended the same junior school in Bristol when Dirac was there, was the much more widely known Archibald Leach, who subsequently changed his name to Cary Grant.

Another member of the group deserving a special mention is **Sir Joseph John Thomson** (1856-1940), who was awarded the Nobel Prize for Physics *"in recognition of the great merits of his theoretical and experimental investigations on the conduction of electricity by gases."* He must have been the most extraordinary teacher. His son was awarded the Nobel Prize for Physics. Six of his research assistants were awarded the Nobel Prize for Physics and two others were awarded the Nobel Prize for Chemistry. His grave is sometimes obscured by the Nave altar as is that of one of his assistants, Ernest Rutherford.

Somewhere in this area is the unmarked grave of **William Cockburn** (1669-1739), a Scottish physician. He joined the Navy and spent time as a ship's surgeon before being appointed Physician to the Blue Squadron. Dining on board a warship one evening somebody observed that what was most needed in the Navy was a cure for dysentry. Cockburn had already come up with a secret remedy for the condition and said that he thought he could help. On the following day an experiment was conducted on between 70 and 80 patients aboard *HMS Sandwich*, which was moored nearby. The experiment was a stunning success and resulted in **Sir Cloudesley Shovell** (1650-1707)[9] being instructed by the Board of Admiralty to acquire sufficient quantities of the remedy to meet the needs of his fleet. Cockburn made his fortune supplying the Fleet for the next 40 years.

Walking back up the Central Aisle of the Nave we come to the grave of **Thomas Cochrane**, 10th Earl of Dundonald (1775-1860), which is depicted overleaf. A very successful frigate captain during the Napoleonic Wars, he and his exploits formed the inspiration for the novels about **Hornblower** (CS Forester) and **Jack Aubrey** (Patrick O'Brien). He caused significant damage to a large section of the Napoleonic fleet in 1809, acting almost single-handedly. Cochrane was a difficult man, who, by criticising the widespread nepotism and corruption in the Admiralty, made many enemies among the powers-that-be. His extraordinary success no doubt gave rise to much jealousy amongst his contemporaries.

In 1814 Cochrane was convicted of a City share fraud (thought by some to have been a trumped up charge) and sent to prison for a year, losing all his honours. Having served his sentence he was approached by **Bernardo O'Higgins** (1778-1842) and asked if he would lead the Chilean Navy in that country's struggle for independence. His successes there led to him achieving heroic status in Chile, recognised today by an annual wreath-laying service in the Abbey attended by representatives of the Chilean Navy. Having helped with Chile he moved up to Peru doing more of the same and then the Brazilians appointed him head of their Imperial Navy to help free them from the Portuguese. That done, the Greeks recruited

---

9   memorialized in the South Choir Aisle

Thomas Cochrane

him for help in their struggle for independence. He returned home a hero and recovered all his lost honours, ending up with the rank of Admiral of the Red.

Moving further west and passing over such luminaries as John Harrison, Thomas Tompion and David Livingstone we come to a stone commemorating the United States financier and philanthropist, **George Peabody** (1795-1869), who was buried here for a short period before being taken back to Massachusetts. On Queen Victoria's instructions his body was taken back on a British warship in recognition of his extraordinary philanthropic generosity towards the poor of London. He founded the organisation now known as "Peabody", a housing association housing more than 70,000 people, mainly in the Greater London area. He was the first United States citizen to be awarded the Freedom of the City of London. From the late 1830s he worked in the City of London selling American bonds, trading under his own name. In 1854 he took in a partner, Junius S Morgan, and when Peabody retired in 1864, Morgan took over and changed the name to JS Morgan & Co, later to become JP Morgan.

Next we come to the **Grave of the Unknown Warrior** about which much has been written. It is the only grave in the Abbey at floor level upon which nobody is permitted to walk and it is always surrounded by replica poppies, the symbol of remembrance devised by Moina Michael, "the Poppy Lady".

She came up with the idea in 1918, inspired by John McCrae's poem *"In Flanders Fields"* and particularly the poem's concluding lines:

> *"To you from failing hands we throw the Torch; be yours to hold it high. If ye break faith with us who die, we shall not sleep, though poppies grow in Flanders Fields".*

She pledged to herself that thereafter she would always wear a red silk poppy to keep faith with those who died. She was instrumental in getting various organisations to follow her example, culminating in the National American Legion in 1920 and the British Legion in 1921.

Looking south from here we can see the Abbot's Pew, an addition provided by Abbot John Islip at the beginning of the 16th century. Above it is the **Royal Flying Corps window**, which was presented by Mrs Louis Bennett of West Virginia. Her son, Louis Bennett Jr., was a pilot in the West Virginia Flying Corps, who came across to England to fight in the First World War. He joined the Royal Flying Corps and was killed. His mother approached the Dean requesting that she be permitted to put up a memorial in her son's honour. The Dean replied that that would not be possible, but that what she could do was to erect a memorial for all those who died flying for the Royal Flying Corps. This window is the result and the face of the figure holding the white shield with the red cross is a portrait of her son.

Below the Abbot's Pew is the memorial to **William Congreve** (1670-1729) who is buried nearby. He had a scandalous affair with Henrietta Godolphin, in her own right **Duchess of Marlborough** (1681-1733)[10], daughter of the famous general, the 1st Duke of Marlborough. Congreve left all his money to Henrietta, who was responsible for erecting his memorial. She also composed the inscription, which refers to the happiness and honour she derived from his company. On seeing the inscription her mother commented that while she could not speak for the happiness she was certain that there was no honour in the relationship. Henrietta's father was buried for a short while in the Ormond vault in Henry VII's chapel, but his remains were subsequently removed to Blenheim. Henrietta gave firm instructions that her remains were to stay in the Abbey.

Next to Congreve is the monument to **Dr John Freind** (1675-1728), the friend of Richard Mead (*supra*), the Jacobite sympathiser who was incarcerated for a time in the Tower. One thing that led to his incarceration was his close association with **Dean Atterbury** (1663-1732), who was exiled to France in 1722.

---

10   also buried in the South Aisle of the Nave

RFC window extract depicting Louis Bennett

William Congreve

Following Atterbury's death in 1732, his body was brought back and buried near where we are standing.

A few paces eastwards we find a small stone marking the grave of **Anne Oldfield** (1683-1730). She became the leading actress of the day, much of her career being spent at Drury Lane. There was a fair amount of rivalry among the leading actresses, Anne's principal competitor at that time being the well-established and very popular **Anne Bracegirdle** (1671-1748)[11]. A competition between Oldfield and Bracegirdle was arranged in 1707. It was agreed that Thomas Betterton's *The Amorous Widow* would be put on for two consecutive nights with Bracegirdle in the leading role on the first night and Oldfield in the same role the second night. It is said that Oldfield was "universally adjudged" the winner, which resulted in Bracegirdle retiring from the theatre. Oldfield became an A-list celebrity and at her death was afforded the privilege of a 'lying in state' in the Abbey's Jerusalem Chamber, but a request that she be permitted a monument was refused by the Dean.

A couple of bays along, we find on the wall of the fourth bay a bust of **William Buckland** (1784-1856), Dean of Westminster from 1845. He was a noted scientist, a Fellow of the Royal Society and twice President of the Geological Society. He was also a noted eccentric, keeping in his house an extraordinary menagerie including snakes, eagles and monkeys. Like many scientists of his day he was not averse to extreme levels of experimentation. *"While dining out one evening at Lord Harcourt's residence at Nuneham in 1848 Buckland was shown a silver locket containing an object resembling pumice stone. He popped the object in his mouth, perhaps to try and find out what mineral it was, and swallowed it. It was in fact part of the mummified heart of Louis XIV of France, which had been taken from the royal tomb by a member of the Harcourt family."[12]*

---

11   buried in the East Cloister

12   quote from Westminster Abbey website

William Buckland

George Wade

Above the West Cloister door, is a memorial to **Field Marshal George Wade** (1673-1748), God's gift to the Scottish tourist industry, buried in the Nave. He was a distinguished soldier who fought in the Nine

Years' War, the War of the Spanish Succession, both Jacobite risings and the War of the Austrian Succession. However he is probably best known now for his military roads, which criss-crossed the Scottish Highlands to facilitate military movement and which now enable tourists to enjoy the full breadth of Scotland. His memorial by Louis Francois Roubiliac was regarded by the sculptor as his finest work. The sculptor was most upset that it was placed so high up the wall.

The roads started off with the 60 mile stretch from Inverness to Fort William, followed in the decade from 1725-1735 with a further 240 miles of road and over 30 bridges including the five-arch bridge over the Tay at Aberfeldy. In the mid-18th century, the song that is now the National Anthem had an occasional additional verse reading;

Lord, grant that Marshal Wade,
May by thy mighty aid,
Victory bring.
May he sedition hush,
and like a torrent rush,
Rebellious Scots to crush,
God save the King.

On the wall in the next bay to the east are two monuments to wives of the writer and mathematician **Sir Samuel Morland** (1625-1695). He composed the inscriptions and was evidently keen to show off his linguistic talents. The inscriptions are in Hebrew, Greek and English on Carola's memorial and in Hebrew, Ge'ez (the classical language of Ethiopia) and English on Ann's memorial. The inscriptions are said to contain many errors stemming from the fact that the letter cutter would not have been familiar with some of those languages.

In the next bay we find a dramatic monument to **Lt-General William Hargrave** (1672-1751). He had been a distinguished soldier and ended up as Governor of Gibraltar, but it is the nature of the monument, which is of particular interest, rather than the deceased. The monument by **Louis Francois Roubiliac** (1702-1762) features themes of Death (the angel in the clouds sounding the last trumpet), the Resurrection (Hargrave emerging naked from his coffin) and the End of Time symbolised by the collapsing pyramid. Much of the monument is painted stone to give the illusion of depth and perspective.

On the same wall is a memorial to the Cornishman, **Sidney Godolphin**, 1st Earl of Godolphin. (1645-1712) He held several high government posts in the late 17th century and early 18th century and helped negotiate and oversee the passing of the Act of Union. He was the father-in-law of William Congreve's intimate friend, Henrietta Godolphin, Duchess of Marlborough, and it was she who paid for the erection of his monument.

William Hargrave

29

Our next and final stop is **Major John André** (1750-1780), whose memorial is on the wall of the last bay before the South Choir Aisle and whose remains lie in the floor nearby a few yards to the west. He joined the army in 1771 and went to North America in 1774; he participated in several of the battles in the War of Independence and rose to the rank of major in 1778 on being appointed deputy adjutant-general.

In that post, André was required to handle the communications between the commander-in-chief (Sir Henry Clinton) and the American spies, one of whom was Benedict Arnold. On 21 September 1780, at dead of night, he went up the Hudson river to meet Arnold. At that meeting Arnold handed over to André all details of the defences of the fort at West Point, but on his return André was arrested by American militiamen and the incriminating material handed to him by Arnold was discovered. He was in civilian clothing and so classed as a spy rather than a soldier and qualified for death by hanging.

He petitioned General Washington to be shot as a soldier, but his request was refused and he was hanged. The memorial depicts a firing squad on the right and a group of people pleading with Washington for either his release or the firing squad. His body was disinterred 40 years later at the instance of the Royal Family for burial in the Abbey. The box in which his remains were brought back survives, but is not on display to the public.

The shields in the bay above André are those of **Richard, Earl of Cornwall, King of the Romans** (1209-1272), Henry III's younger brother, and the Earl of Ross. Henry gave Cornwall to his brother for a birthday present.

John André

Acknowledgments

The author is grateful to the Dean and Chapter of Westminster for provision of the photographs *(Copyright the Dean and Chapter of Westminster)* and for the editorial assistance provided by Christine Reynolds, Assistant Keeper of the Muniments, James Rawlinson, Volunteer Coordinator and my stalwart editorial masterminds, Buffy Moyse and Rupert Hill.

Sources

The Abbey website, **www.westminster-abbey.org**

Dean Stanley's Historical Memorials of Westminster Abbey

The Oxford Dictionary of National Biography